Freedom's Design:
20 Days of Empowering Black Kings
I Am My History

By: Brian Keith Harris II

Volume I
2019

Editorial and Design: Joy L. King
Cover Design: CoLab Creative Group
Poetry: Brian Keith Harris II
Published by: Brian Keith Harris II

Printed by Kindle Direct Publishing, in the United States of America.

ISBN: 978-0-578-54395-6

First printing, 2019.

For more information, visit:
www.briankeithharris.com
briankharris02@gmail.com

Dedication

This book is dedicated to my grandmother, the late Artie Jean Weathers, a true woman of God, who always prayed for me. Her words of encouragement and prayers became anthems that prepared me for my journey and inspired this book.

I hope to honor her legacy and the sacrifices she made for my family, by continuing to positively impact the lives of boys of color.

Grandma, I love you, I miss you, and I am grateful for your presence in my life.

Table of Contents

Week Four: Black Boy Rising

Foreword

Unfortunately, the plight of black boys continues to be precarious. They are still the canaries in the mine. The societal environment in which they live continues to be a toxic ecosystem that poses threats to their opportunity to survive and thrive.

Too often, black boys are deemed a menace to society - dangerous merely because of their presence or appearance. *The Look*, a brief video produced by Proctor and Gamble, showed what too many black boys experience when they are browsing in a high end store or entering an elevator being the sole black face. The look that they receive silently says, "what are you doing here? You don't belong here!" As the canary in the mine, black boys experience the first fumes of racism and stereotypes. They are routinely subjected to assaults on their self-esteem and self-worth.

Fortunately, *Freedom's Design: 20 Days of Empowering Black Kings* has come to their rescue. This powerful book of affirmations written by Brian Harris charts a course that affirms the genius that rests ready to be unleashed within each black boy. Brian Harris is an educator, mentor, hope-dealer, mentor and teacher of dance. Brian is an amazing purveyor of energy and innovation. His demonstrable zeal has afforded him the magic touch to create the "secret sauce" designed to make hopes, dreams, and aspirations attainable.

Bound within the pages of *Freedom's Design: 20 Days of Empowering Black Kings* are affirmations that are sure to last a lifetime and leave indelible imprints on the lives of black boys who read and soak in their inspiration. This book is sure to provide black boys with a powerful antidote against the toxins of bias, stereotypes, low expectations, and societal poisons which threaten their social, emotional, cultural and academic development.

In my 50 years as an educator, I can attest to the power of affirmations and their ability to heal the soul and spirit of black boys. *Freedom's Design: 20 Days of Empowering Black Kings* will inoculate the reader with confidence, resiliency, and identity reinforcement. The book is written with the clear intent to become the North Star that black boys use to navigate the pathway to success.

Just as Harriet Tubman led hundreds through the Underground Railroad, so will *Freedom's Design: 20 days of Empowering Black Kings* liberate our sons from the shackles of cultural mis-education. It has my unequivocal endorsement.

Ron Walker
Founding Executive Director
Coalition of Schools Educating Boys of Color

Dear Young Black King,

Welcome! The next 20 days will be an amazing journey of empowerment, education, and inspiration. This book will teach you about your rich history and legacy, challenge you to push through obstacles, and show you how to be a shining example for your community and the world. This book will help you to become the person you have been created to be and give you the tools needed to achieve success in every area of your life. You are filled with infinite power and light and it is time for the world to see the potential you have within.

I wrote this book to help you see yourself as a King and not be a slave to the stigmas and stereotypes of society. I wrote this book to give you a glimpse of the tenacity and strength our ancestors possessed in their fight for justice and equality and how those same qualities are present inside of you. I wrote this book to help you gain the courage necessary to step beyond mediocrity and push the boundaries of your own creativity. I wrote this book so that you could have a space to express yourself and share your thoughts about the injustices in our society and think about what you can do to create change.

It is my sincere hope that as you read through the pages, you will find the true meaning of "Black Boy Joy," and it will encourage you to dream big and soar high!

Be sure to take advantage of the reflection questions and affirmations, as it will help to extend your learning and heighten your level of awareness and "dopeness."

With Love and Light,
Brian

You are a Black King

You are a Black King, with courage to incite change,
to be extraordinary and not just mediocre or mundane.

You are a Black King, with power to break free,
from the chains that guard you and control your destiny.

You are a Black King with creativity to transform,
Innovation is in your DNA from the day you were born.

You are a Black King with the potential to heal,
the cries of your community you understand and feel.

You are a Black King with a history so great,
You can write your narrative and determine your fate.

You are a Black King so soar high above the sky,
it's your time to take the wind and begin to fly.

The King's Commitment

I _____ (insert name) will embrace this moment of learning about my history and rich legacy. I will honor this space of freedom and creativity and I am grateful for an opportunity to share, express and discuss my thoughts and feelings with my peers.

This moment is an opportunity for me to explore and experience freedom in a new way and I commit to invest 100% of my energy, attention and self for the next 20 days.

I AM A KING!

Sign Your Name:

_____

In the space below, draw a symbol that represents who you are, or want to become in the future.

Week One: I am MY History

I am my History. I have the courage to walk tall and stand in royalty.

Today, I will behave like a King, with respect, dignity and confidence.

Day 1

I am MY History

I am MY history
Walking tall
Standing in royalty
I am a direct descendant of kings and queens who ruled with grace,
wisdom and dignity.

I Am MY history
A designer
A thinker
A being of creativity
I built the pyramids of Egypt with my strength and agility
I mastered Math and Science, so brilliantly

I am MY history
A child of the diaspora
A survivor of slavery
For 400 years I fought to be free
Escaping the hands of hatred and captivity

I AM a powerful source of peace
I AM a brave beautiful light
I AM essential to Earth
I AM the glimmering hope in the darkness of night

I am MY History
The injustices of the world didn't stop me
I overcame obstacles and beat adversity

I stood up like Martin, Rosa, and Jackie

I AM a vision of MY ancestors
I AM a symbol of LOVE
I AM God's greatest creation
I AM a gift from above

I am MY history
Walking tall, standing in royalty
I will continue this legacy knowing
that nothing can STOP ME!

Day One Reflection...

Imagine you are a King of your own empire. What are three principles your empire will live by and why are these principles important?

_____
_____
_____
_____
_____
_____
_____
_____
_____
_____
_____
_____
_____
_____
_____
_____
_____
_____
_____
_____
_____
_____
_____

Day 2

Africa, My Homeland

Sounds of Africa,
Whispering throughout the wind
Lifting me higher.

Drums of Africa,
Beating in my soulful heart
Let the rhythm speak.

Mother Africa,
Her strength flows like the bright sun
Her love is my home.

Day Two Reflection...

What kind of activity could you create to celebrate African culture at your school?

_____

_____

_____

_____

_____

_____

_____

_____

_____

_____

_____

_____

_____

_____

_____

_____

_____

_____

_____

_____

_____

_____

_____

_____

Dancing with the Drumbeat

Da Da Diddie Da Da Da
Da Da Diddie Da Da Da

The drumbeat in my feet is piercing my soul,
It is the center of life for my people, young and old.

Da Da Diddie Da Da Da
Da Da Diddie Da Da Da

The drumbeat in my feet brings me laughter and joy,
It is the symbol of hope for every girl and boy.

Da Da Diddie Da Da Da
Da Da Diddie Da Da Da

The drumbeat in my feet makes me feel good inside,
Mother Africa kisses me with her sun and opens her arms wide.

Da Da Diddie Da Da Da
Da Da Diddie Da Da Da

Day Three Reflection...

What are some benefits of dance? How does dancing make you feel?

_____

_____

_____

_____

_____

_____

_____

_____

_____

_____

_____

_____

_____

_____

_____

_____

_____

_____

_____

_____

_____

_____

_____

_____

_____

Don't Call Me Out of My Name

I'm working hard to find my real last name,
the one I have is not my own.
It was given to my African family during slavery,
when the truth of who they were wasn't shown.

I'm working hard to find my real last name,
the one I have just doesn't fit me.
It is a name disconnected from my heritage,
given to my people who couldn't break free.

I'm working hard to find my real last name,
My culture was stripped from me,
My people are from Ghana, Mali, and Senegal
whose last names are in Yoruba, Wolof, and even Twi.

Africa, the motherland,
The place where my history began.
Where my skin was kissed by the Sun,
Brown, black, red and tan.

The place that gave me high cheekbones
and my beautiful wide smile,
the place where freedom roams
and being different is in style.

I'm working hard to find my real last name,
you should join me on my quest.
There is joy in knowing from where you have come,
for it will help you to achieve greatness.

9

Day Four Reflection...

Research 3 important facts about each of the African countries in the poem. What are some similarities among the countries? Which country most represents you? Why?

_____

_____

_____

_____

_____

_____

_____

_____

_____

_____

_____

_____

_____

_____

_____

_____

_____

_____

_____

_____

_____

_____

_____

_____

_____

Day 5

Rest in Peace or Remain in Power

A stray bullet can kill you,
Not knowing your history can too.
You can die from the loss of blood or lack of knowledge, both will extinguish you.

A bullet has no name on it, but history has names on a list of people who pushed through barriers, who have the marks of handcuffs imprinted on their wrists.

When you don't know your history, you become a target for them all - your future becomes blurry, and your dreams begin to fall.

But when you know your history, you have power that comes from within, that holds you up when leaning and whispers, "Get up and try again."

We must take time to learn about those who paved the way, whose shadows we walk in, whose shoulders we stand on every day.

We must make a vow that no matter what's going on, we will speak their names in every lyric and in every song.

The predators of prejudice have good aim, so study your history, shielding yourself with these names.

Harriet Tubman
Martin Luther King Jr.
Ella Baker, too
History will be revealed, but is waiting on YOU.

Day Five Reflection...

Why is it important to learn your history?

_____

_____

_____

_____

_____

_____

_____

_____

_____

_____

_____

_____

_____

_____

_____

_____

_____

_____

_____

_____

_____

_____

_____

_____

_____

_____

_____

_____

Week Two: Freedom Fighters

I am a black king with courage. Today, I will fight and stand up for my freedom!

Day 6

Freedom Fighters

They said we couldn't do it; we marched.
They tried to keep us from it; we marched.

They turned on the fire hoses; we resisted.
They brought out the vicious dogs; we persisted.

They instituted Jim Crow; we protested.
They said we couldn't vote; we contested.

Sister Angela Davis spoke out for us,
Brother James Farmer told us to "Get on the bus."
Sister Assata Shakur made a righteous fuss.
Brother Stokely Carmichael wasn't scared enough!

They shouted Nigger; we screamed, "Black is beautiful."
They stole our opportunities, we still became fruitful.

Day Six Reflection...

How do you think it would feel to live during segregation?

_____

_____

_____

_____

_____

_____

_____

_____

_____

_____

_____

_____

_____

_____

_____

_____

_____

_____

_____

_____

_____

_____

_____

_____

_____

_____

_____

_____

Day 7

Every Time I Feel the Spirit

The spirit of my ancestral Mothers brings joy to my feet
Every time I feel them something happens inside of me
It appears to be a mystery, I can't quite describe,
I'm knocked out of my seat and my hands lift up high!

Perhaps it's Mother Harriet Tubman or Mother Coretta Scott King,
whose spirit of courage lets my freedom ring.

Maybe it's Mother Fannie Lou Hamer or Mother Dorothy Height,
whose spirit of strength lifts my wings in flight.

It could be Mother Zora Neal Hurston or Mother Billie Holiday
whose spirit of creativity illuminates my way.

It is clear to me now why these women move me
Their gifts made it possible for me to live freely
Igniting my passion and daring me to dream
A son of these Mothers, whose presence is real.

Day Seven Reflection...

Think about a woman who has impacted your life in a positive way (ex. mother, teacher, family member). Write a letter to her about her contributions to your life.

_____

_____

_____

_____

_____

_____

_____

_____

_____

_____

_____

_____

_____

_____

_____

_____

_____

_____

_____

_____

_____

_____

_____

_____

_____

Day 8

Echoes from Emmett

Frustrated, one summer afternoon, I sat under an oak tree being still
When suddenly a voice spoke to me and said, "Hello. I am Emmett Till.

My journey began in 1941, Chicago was the place of my birth,
but in 1955 at the age of 14, I tragically left this Earth.
I was awakened from sleep that hot Mississippi night,
And taken from my family without putting up a fight.

My body was brutally beaten, a shot to the head took my breath away,
I was thrown into the river, never to live another day.

I am here to encourage you to keep achieving your dreams,
You gotta keep on moving, even when you want to scream.
Don't allow hatred to silence your voice,
Speak up and let love ALWAYS be your choice."

I walked away from that tree with Emmett's words resonating peacefully
Grateful for my own life and releasing small frustrations easily.

Day Eight Reflection…

Imagine you are a young man growing up in the 1950s during segregation, what might be some of your fears? How might you handle discrimination?

_____

_____

_____

_____

_____

_____

_____

_____

_____

_____

_____

_____

_____

_____

_____

_____

_____

_____

_____

_____

_____

_____

_____

_____

_____

Day 9

Maya, Martin, and Me

Maya Angelou gave voice to those who couldn't speak

Activating their truth and allowing their souls to be free

You could count on her to promote love and harmony

A true warrior for justice, whose light shines eternally

Martin Luther King Jr. was a man of faith

A civil rights leader for the human race

Righteousness guided him to a peaceful place

Taught us how to take up equal space

Inspired a movement with humility and grace

Now it's our time to end inequality and be the face

Many African-Americans made it possible for me to pursue my dreams and reach my destiny.

Every time I think of the path they paved for me, I get excited about my life's journey and my rich legacy.

Day Nine Reflection…

Is civil disobedience (disobeying an unjust law) ever acceptable?
Why or why not?

_____

_____

_____

_____

_____

_____

_____

_____

_____

_____

_____

_____

_____

_____

_____

_____

_____

_____

_____

_____

_____

_____

Black Wall Street

There was a district of businesses called Black Wall Street,
Where entrepreneurs created tables of wealth and took their seats.

Tulsa, Oklahoma was the place where it all began,
a development of wealth for every black woman and man.

Where people weren't afraid to pursue their dreams,
no matter how challenging it became or how difficult it seemed.

Those 36 businesses all in one row,
were bombed in 1921 because of Jim Crow.

Trying to help the culture be financially free,
Black Wall Street is now a distant memory.

Start a business to build up your community,
use your divine gifts to claim financial victory.

Day Ten Reflection...

Imagine you own a business. What is the name of your business? How will it help the community? Create a logo that represents your business.

_____

_____

_____

_____

_____

_____

_____

_____

_____

Draw Your Logo Here:

Week Three: For the Culture

There is no time to waste. Today, I will do what is necessary in order to become successful in school, at home and in life.

Just Do It

Do it for the culture, not for the Gram,
Stop allowing the likes to define you, fam.

Do it for Trayvon Martin, do it for Michael Brown,
You're a King young man, adjust your crown.

Do it for the people who marched for civil rights,
Do it for those who decided to fight.
Do it for the books they were not allowed to read,

Do it for the blood that you don't have to bleed.
Do it for the life you were designed to live,
Do it for your freedom, give it all you can give.

Just Do It.

Day Eleven Reflection...

What do you dream of becoming in life? How can you start accomplishing that dream today?

_____

_____

_____

_____

_____

_____

_____

_____

_____

_____

_____

_____

_____

_____

_____

_____

_____

_____

_____

_____

_____

_____

_____

_____

One Knee

I'm taking one knee with Colin and I don't care what they say,
man, I'm tired of being treated this way.

I'm taking one knee with Colin, cause' it just ain't fair
my brothers are being killed and no one seems to care.

I'm taking one knee with Colin, and that's a fact,
like when Coretta Scott King marched and Rosa Parks sat.

I'm taking one knee with Colin, it's time we stand up for what's right,
with persistence and resistance we can win this fight.

I'm taking one knee with Colin and I hope you will too,
the elders of our history are rooting for me and you.

Day Twelve Reflection...

What is something you stood up for in the past? Describe the experience.

_____

_____

_____

_____

_____

_____

_____

_____

_____

_____

_____

_____

_____

_____

_____

_____

_____

_____

_____

_____

_____

_____

_____

_____

_____

_____

Social Media

You scroll up and down your timeline throughout the entire day,
Waiting for a *like* or a comment thrown your way.
Somehow the number of followers and likes determine your worth,
Instead of the fact you are breathing on Earth.

You say, "It's social media bruh, chill out. It ain't that deep."
And I say, "It is defining who you are, it's even controlling your sleep."
Social Media is that hurricane that has taken the world by storm,
It has washed our children in the river of filters, their image now reborn.

Day Thirteen Reflection...

Imagine social media was shut down for good. How might not having a Facebook, Instagram, Snapchat or Twitter profile page affect you? Do you think social media has the power to change people? Why or why not?

_____

_____

_____

_____

_____

_____

_____

_____

_____

_____

_____

_____

_____

_____

_____

_____

_____

_____

_____

_____

_____

_____

_____

_____

Dear Black Boy

Dear Black Boy,
Rise up
Put on your crown, King
It is your time to shine.

Dear Black Boy,
Fly high
Soar into your destiny
On the wings of your ancestors.

Dear Black Boy,
Stay Strong
Be confident and courageous
Create change in the world.

Day Fourteen Reflection...

Imagine you opened your own school for black boys. What are 5 essential values your school will promote? How will you ensure the success of your students?

_____
_____
_____
_____
_____
_____
_____
_____
_____
_____
_____
_____
_____
_____
_____
_____
_____
_____
_____
_____
_____
_____
_____
_____
_____

The Power of 12

Potential
Purpose
Persistence
Promise

These gifts are getting ready to be released on Earth.
It is YOU that will usher in the arrival, giving black and brown boys new birth.

Courage
Confidence
Charisma
Creativity

These gifts are getting ready to set the world ablaze.
It is YOU that will start this trend, the power of your vibration will make waves.

Love
Light
Leadership
Legacy

These gifts will turn the world upside down.
It is YOU that will bring hope to us all, allowing healing and peace to be found.

Day Fifteen Reflection...

Write a 12-line poem that describes what kind of world in which you want to live.

_____

_____

_____

_____

_____

_____

_____

_____

_____

_____

_____

_____

_____

_____

_____

_____

_____

_____

_____

_____

_____

_____

_____

_____

_____

Week Four: Black Boy Rising

My future is bright and full of promise. Today, I will be present in this moment that defines my destiny.

Day 16

Reflections and Affirmations of a Black Boy

I wake up in the morning, discovering a new version of myself, a reflection of those who have gone on before me.

I lift my hands to the bright sun, thanking the elders for endowing me with the power to hold fast to my dreams.

I open my eyes and see the love that is all around me and the strength to overcome every obstacle that stands in my way.

Each day that I live, each moment that I breathe, I am becoming the man I was created to be.

I am a light shining through the darkness, illuminating the path for my brothers who will come after me.

I know my future is bright and full of promise, and I choose to be present in this moment that defines my destiny.

Day Sixteen Reflection...

What is your hope for black boys in the future? What do you want them to always remember?

_____

_____

_____

_____

_____

_____

_____

_____

_____

_____

_____

_____

_____

_____

_____

_____

_____

_____

_____

_____

_____

_____

_____

_____

Day 17

I Press

I press toward my goals and dreams,
despite how hard the road may seem.

I press toward my future and continue to thrive,
through the darkness of night I will survive.

I press toward a place of peace,
where my fears are silenced and my worries released.

I press toward a life filled with peace and joy,
Where there is equity for every girl and boy.

I press toward the change of stories told,
And black and brown boys get to grow old.

Day Seventeen Reflection...

What is something you are pressing to achieve? How will accomplishing this goal help your community?

_____

_____

_____

_____

_____

_____

_____

_____

_____

_____

_____

_____

_____

_____

_____

_____

_____

_____

_____

_____

_____

_____

_____

_____

_____

_____

Dear Hatred

Dear Hatred,

You paralyzed me with your vicious attacks,
I can't move without you being on my back.

You snatched the breath from thousands of slaves,
whose voices echo in the distance from their shallow graves.

You ripped the courage out of my chest,
while police officers placed me under arrest.

We are the chosen generation,
We are ready to fight.
We are now stronger than before,
With freedom in our sight.

With our fists in the air,
Our heads to the sky,
We're taking back our freedom
One community at a time.

Signed,
Brave Black Boy

Day Eighteen Reflection...

How can you help to spread love in your school and community?

_____

_____

_____

_____

_____

_____

_____

_____

_____

_____

_____

_____

_____

_____

_____

_____

_____

_____

_____

_____

_____

_____

Day 19

Black Boy Rising

Black Boy stop running
You were created to soar
Spread your wings and fly.

The hands of young Kings
Fighting through the wilderness
Searching for freedom.

Black Sons of freedom
Bringing light to a dark world
Lend your song to me.

Day Nineteen Reflection...

What are 3 life lessons you would share with younger Kings to help them be successful in school and in life?

_____
_____
_____
_____
_____
_____
_____
_____
_____
_____
_____
_____
_____
_____
_____
_____
_____
_____
_____
_____
_____
_____
_____
_____

Day 20

Yes I Can

He raised his hand to give the Presidential oath,
What a wonderful sight to see.
The 44th President of the United States,
Looked just like you and me.

He said, "Voting for ALL,"
So we answered the CALL.

He said, "Yes We Can,"
So we decided to STAND.

He said, "The White House is yours too,"
So we gathered in droves and walked on through.

President Barack Obama gives me hope
For there is a piece of him inside of me.
With hard work and dedication,
I too will help my people and lead.

Yes I Can!

Day Twenty Reflection...

President Barack Obama coined the phrase, "Yes We Can." What would you say to parents, teachers, or principals about how they can help Black Boys to be more successful in life?

_____

_____

_____

_____

_____

_____

_____

_____

_____

_____

_____

_____

_____

_____

_____

_____

_____

_____

_____

_____

_____

_____

_____

_____

Daily Affirmations

A DAILY AFFIRMATION for a King like YOU

I am a strong King with courage to meet this day.

I am AMAZING and BOLD
I am CARING and DETERMINED.

I am a gifted King with creativity to meet this day.

I am ENERGETIC and FEARLESS
I am GRATEFUL and HEALTHY

I am an intelligent King with a bright mind to meet this day.

I am INQUISITIVE and JOYFUL
I am KIND and LOVING

I am an organized King with a plan to meet this day.

I am MINDFUL of others and NOBLE
I am OPTIMISTIC and PHENOMENAL

I am a dedicated King with stamina to meet this day.

I am FORGIVING and RESPECTFUL
I am SUCCESSFUL and TRUSTWORTHY

I am a supportive King with compassion to meet this day.

I am VALORUS and UNIQUE
I am WISE and X-tra DOPE

I am a positive King with peace to meet this day.

I am YOUNG and FULL OF LIFE
I am ZEALOUS and READY TO GO!

An Affirmation for Difficult Days

Today I will try my best,
Despite how I am feeling inside.

Today I will call on my ancestors,
To lead, direct and guide.

Today I will be kind to myself,
No matter what is going on.

Today I will love me,
I will dance and play my favorite song.

Today will pass and a new day will begin,
I am grateful for life and the ability to start again.

10 Affirmations to know as I GROW…

1. Everything I need to be successful I already have.

2. Peace and blessings flow freely to me and through me.

3. I am not perfect, but striving to be my best self.

4. It is okay to make mistakes. It is not okay to allow my mistakes to keep me from my goals and dreams.

5. I am the writer of my story.

6. There is love all around me and I have the ability to embrace it all.

7. Each day that I live, I am becoming more amazing and dope.

8. I have the power to walk away from things that are negative and harmful to my life.

9. Life will not always make sense, but if I keep moving, things will become clearer as the days go by.

10. Breathing and counting to 10, always helps me be calm.

Acknowledgements

To My Family and Friends:
Thanks for enthusiastically supporting me during the writing of this book and in every one of my endeavors in life. You inspired me to press on during the challenging moments and I am grateful for your continued support and love.

Brian and Carla Harris (Mom and Dad):
Thanks for listening attentively during the writing of this book. Your unwavering confidence in me gives me life and fuels my passion to pursue my purpose.

Tina Lee (Sons of Freedom Program Coordinator):
Thanks for always having my back and for listening to every poem in this book! Your unselfishness is golden and your feedback was essential to the project.

Joy L. King (Editor):
Thank you for helping me to write poetry that will transform the lives of black boys and give them hope for a brighter tomorrow. Your patience helped to steer this project and process.

Whitney Hoggans (Book Coach and Mentor):
Thanks for always being a listening ear and for offering your knowledge, skill and expertise to help me find the essence of this work. Your work, love and support is immeasurable.

Ron Walker and Dr. Ron Whitaker (Mentors)
Thanks for being mentors who pour into me consistently and push me to continue impacting the lives of black boys. Your support and confidence in me has been priceless.

About the Author

Brian Keith Harris II is the Director of Outplacement and Graduate Support at the Bishop Walker School for Boys in Washington, DC. He is the Founder and Artistic Director of Sons of Freedom Dance Institute, an organization committed to nurturing character development, increasing social awareness and building a spiritual foundation for boys of color through classical and contemporary styles of dance.

Brian facilitates workshops at professional educational conferences throughout the country that empower educators in urban communities and inspires black and brown boys to gain the tools to change their life's narrative. He has received numerous awards and recognition for his work in education, the arts and in learning and development of young men. In 2019, Brian was named one of Black Enterprise Magazine's BeModern Men of Distinction.

Brian is a doctoral student at Wesley Theological Seminary in Washington, DC where his work explores the intersection of Spirituality and Educational Equity in Urban Communities. He also earned a Master's Degree in Divinity (M.Div) with an emphasis in Christian Education from The Samuel DeWitt Proctor School of Theology and has an undergraduate degree in Print Journalism from Hampton University.

Made in the USA
Columbia, SC
07 December 2019

84503703R00035